Red Flag Series: Starting a New Paranormal Team

Brenda K. Pipo

ISBN: 1475161026
ISBN-13: 978-1475161021

DEDICATION

This is to those who are searching for a place in the paranormal community but have been so frustrated by bogus Paranormal Teams that they decide to form a team themselves.

Believe me when I say….. It's not as easy as you think!

ACKNOWLEDGMENTS

I want to thank my husband, Vic, first and foremost, for those late nights being dragged to "Mystery" locations where he met total strangers and spent all night traipsing around their houses or businesses. He has always supported me in this and been there to help when needed.

Hugs to my Step Kids, Tristan and Rachel, just for being the best.

Next to last but not least, my gratitude and devotion to my paranormal family and partners in crime: Black Wolf Paranormal[1]. Colette and A.J. there are not words enough to express my appreciation.

Finally, to all the Paranormal Teams out there and independent investigators. Keep doing what you're doing. Through all our efforts one day we will be able to scientifically prove these experiences. Perhaps it will actually become Normal and we'll all have to change our team names.

---

[1] http://www.blackwolf-paranormal.com/

Preface

As in many fields there are different ways of doing everything. This is intended as a guide only and a voice to share dos and don'ts in the organization of a paranormal team. The material is based on lessons learned though personal experiences. Every individual and team needs to determine what works for them. We cannot all be a clone of one another nor should we be. It is this variety that will help us to find answers to all of those mysteries.

I'm going to jump on the defensive here at bit because I know what's coming and I can hear some comments now....in many sections you will think I've gone overboard and am making a bid deal out of nothing and wasting paper. My reply, "If you don't think you need to do whatever I'm talking about, then don't do it." I'm not saying you have to do EVERYTHING I state in this guild. What I am providing are SUGGESTED actions. Whether you do all, some or none is your decision. Phew! I feel better now and will get out of defensive mode.

Throughout this guide the joining is referred to as a TEAM instead of a GROUP. The definition of a **group** is "a number of people sharing something in common such as an interest, belief, or political aim" [2] whereas the definition of a **team** is "a number of people organized to function cooperatively as a group"[3]. Anyone can put a group together. When looking at the definition of **team**, the key words to keep in mind here are "organized" and "cooperatively". It takes effort and planning to put a team together.

---

[2] As defined in Encarta Dictionary
[3] As defined in Encarta Dictionary

Introduction

Paranormal investigating and researching is such a large arena that no one individual could possess the ability to cover all areas of interest at all times. The paranormal umbrella covers more than just ghosts. For this reason the establishment of a team is advantageous to all participants. Through a joining, experience and knowledge can be exchanged and not one individual has to be the expert in all subjects.

In perspective, establishing and running a paranormal team is no different from establishing and running a business. You want to make sure you have a firm base with qualified personnel, business processes in place and a quality customer service.

As in business make sure there is paperwork to back every step of your operation and make sure that it is openly available to all employees, in this case team members.

This guide touches on those steps needed to start a Paranormal team but most important, those RED FLAGS.

Red Flags are things to watch out for that may be a signal your Team has possible issues. They are also warnings of things that can happen. Trust me when I say these were learned through experience.

It only took going through two, now non-existent, teams to get it right. There are just some RED FLAGS you can't get over. It was best to start fresh.

Chapter 1. Conception

The first and most important phase is conception. The minute that first idea to start a paranormal team comes into your mind, expectations are being set. You might not realize it but they are. The foundation laid here will be the basis of all future phases.

Purpose

Why do you want to start a team?

There is some reason you got the idea. Whether it was prior experience with another paranormal team and you didn't like the way it was done or something you saw on TV, the trigger for this decision came from somewhere and spurred a need. Why do you want to do this?

Will this be just for social interaction or actual scientific research?

What is the ultimate goal for the team (i.e. TAPS[4] family member, celebrity)?

The purpose of your team is a big deal.
- If you want to develop a team that will strive to positively impact the paranormal field through any number of actions: research, investigations, assisting others, etc - then you're on track. We need more teams seriously documenting and striving to find answers to those things that go bump in the night and to admit when that bump is a branch against a window.

---

[4] The Atlantic Paranormal Society

You have to want to disprove A haunting as much as prove it

- If your reasons are for social interaction with others who think the paranormal is cool, you might want to look into a chat room or just form a social club. Don't limit yourself to the paranormal
- If you dream of getting a television show and just want the celebrity or to be a big shot.... Well......Big Brother and Survivor are casting for next season. This is NOT the route for you

RED FLAGS

- If you want a team but don't see the reasons for taking it seriously. You think it would just be neat to say you belonged to a Paranormal Team. There are those of us that take this seriously. Every bogus team out there makes it harder for us to gain respect in the paranormal community and with the public in general. Get a life!
- If you are thinking you can make money on this. Wrong! Most teams do what they do voluntarily. There is no pay for this. However, there is a lot of gratification and you can meet some wonderful people....... Some nut cases also, but mostly great people

Effort

Do you find you don't have enough hours in the day now to do what you want to do? Paranormal investigation and participation in a team is time consuming and requires dedication.

You need to ask yourself two very important questions:

> How much of your time and effort are you willing to put into establishing a Team?

> How much time and effort are you willing to put into after it has been established?

The amount of time an investigation alone takes is a big chunk. We're talking anywhere from 4-12+ hours. Now, multiply that by how many devices you have recording: audio, video, etc. For example a 5 hour investigation with 4 DVR cameras, 4 audio recorders, 1 handheld video camera and assorted digital cameras will total at least:

∇ 5 hours – actual investigation

∇ 20+ hours – review of 4 DVR cameras. When you see something out of the ordinary you will most likely replay this over and over. Therefore it will take more than the 20 hours of recording time

∇ 20+ hours – review of audio recorders. When you hear something out of the ordinary you will most likely replay this over and over. Therefore it will take more than the 20 hours of recording time

∇ 5+ hours - review of video camera. Same as with the DVR cameras. You will most likely stop the video multiple times to review footage.

∇ 2 hours – estimated review (at a minimum) of digital photos

Total – over 52 hours for the investigation and evidence review.

Now that doesn't count the customer contact before and after the investigation, the research before and after the investigation regarding the location and any other area happenings, equipment prep, team meetings, etc.

AND... that's just for the investigations. There are so many other things that take time, effort and willingness. That's a whole different guide. Granted you will have your team members to help. But this is a team and all members must assist with all tasks. One person should not be expected to do it all, nor do you want them to.

The more people that review the same evidence the better. You might miss something that another member would catch. Therefore, just because someone else is already doing something won't mean you shouldn't be. That's more time out of your everyday life.

It is a lifestyle change to take this on and be successful, both you and the team. Your family life will be changed whether you intend it to or not.

RED FLAG

- Don't have time for 30 minute chores now? You more than likely won't be able to set aside 1 or more hours a week to be on a team let alone head one

Standards and Requirements

There may be specific principles, ethical standards and/or requirements that are important to you and you insist the resulting team abide by.   During this phase you need to have these finalized and documented.   In later phases these will help to mold what becomes the final organization.   If not set in stone here they will be open for discussion and decision later by the team where the results may differ from what you envision.   Remember, you also have to be willing and able to stand up for what you dictate.

The following are examples of topics that will come up as your decision now or under ESTABLISHMENT, once other members have joined.   For additional information see the associated topics under Chapter 3. ESTABLISHMENT.

- Dues vs. no dues
- Rules of Membership – Code of Conduct and penalties associated with violations
- Mission Statement
- Legal rules – client liability, team liability, member contract
- Team publicity – web site, etc.
- Meeting frequency
- Democratic infrastructure vs. dictatorship
- Evidence Ownership

The easy way to start on this is by asking yourself after each topic:

What is important to me?

RED FLAGS

- As a founder, if you don't know what you want out of this, how can you put together a team of people that share your expectations? This is something YOU need to understand and have outlined so that it doesn't turn into something you never intended it to
- Don't assume that being founder will ensure your decisions will be adhered to unquestionably. There will always be those personalities that will question anything and everything. This is more reason why you need to document and make your wishes, standards and requirements, very clear at the beginning
- Once your team has been established and as founder, being wishy-washy regarding standards and requirements will quickly deflate confidence in your leadership

How do I formally document my standards and requirements?

You're decisions should be documented and clarified in the Mission Statement, By-Laws and Rules of Membership. These are covered in the associated topics under Chapter 3. Establishment.

Chapter 2. Personnel

People are your biggest resource and your reason for having a team. Without people there could be no team. So, to say the least, this is VERY important. With this comes a difficult chore: How to make a group of people get along well enough to operate as a team that trusts one another with their lives[5] and can communicate. It's hard enough to find a spouse fitting these criteria let alone several people.

Remember from the Preface, that definition of Team: a number of people organized to function cooperatively as a group. Keep this in mind as you answer these questions:

How many members should you have?
What does being a member mean?
How do you select members?
Who does what?
Agreeing to Disagree?

RED FLAG

- Simply said, people change. Understanding and accepting this fact will make the going a little easier. You will find in many cases your tolerance level will increase as you get attached to some members and decrease as you get to know others.

Like you, they have other things going on in their lives that will impact the team in one way or another. How you respond to these members as they go through these life trials will either earn you appreciative and dedicated members or frustrated and disgruntled members.

---

[5] On an investigation, your team mate may be your connection to safety.

Large Team vs. Small Team

This is a hard call. Although having a large team definitely helps with the manpower issues, it also brings in more personalities and potentially more issues.

With a large team it is possible to do two investigations at the same time by having sub-teams assigned to each client. The more members the more input on evidence reviews. In general, with more individuals comes more experience for the team.

Now... here comes the BUT...if your investigations are few and far between and they involve residences it might be hard to choose who gets to go and who doesn't, therefore causing hurt feelings. Many residential investigations involve a small area and teams of 2-3 people are more than adequate. You don't want 15 team members encroaching on a small family. It's not only intimidating to the family but also defeats the purpose of trying to maintain a controlled environment.

Having to tell members they can't go on investigations is not easy. Perhaps that is something the team will have to decide regarding how it is determined which members do attend investigations.

There really is no right answer for this other than what works for you. Start small and add members until the team feels it is balanced.

Some teams have opted for membership levels where there are active members and those that just want to belong. Again, it is what works for you. Just have it documented.

RED FLAGS

- The more people you have the more personalities you have to conflict and contend with
- Client locations will limit the number of members on an investigation
- Too many members on an investigation could contaminate evidence making creating a controlled environment close to impossible

Team Name & Logo

If you are totally set on calling the team a certain name, put that down in writing and glue it down. Do the same with the logo.

Team names come from all aspects of life. Some sound like extremely serious fraternal organizations while others may just as well be the name of a roller derby team. Again, same thing applies with logos.

On the other hand, if the team name and/or logo is of little matter to you, save that as a team decision to be made with your charter team members.

As with Black Wolf Paranormal (BWP)[6], the team I'm on now and will be forever, it is named in honor of a beloved companion to one of the founders. Whereas my second attempt at a team – pre-BWP, had us called "Conscious Paranormal".

---

[6] Black Wolf Paranormal can be found at http://www.blackwolf-paranormal.com/

Yep! I take all the credit for that one. Have no idea where it came from or why. Just was different. The logo was the Northern Lights with the name over them.

RED FLAGS

- Use the internet to make sure there are no other teams using the same name you want to use or the logo. Best not to go using another name already established. There are several reasons, good and bad. Basically you don't want to be confused with another team. Your team will be judged by its reputation. You want to earn that yourself and not acquire the reputation of another team
- Just a personal comment..... keep it clean, both name and logo. In this field you work with families and kids a lot. I've seen cases where a team was not called because the family was offended by the team name. It was sad because the team members were really nice and they did good work. I know you can't please everyone but there is a point where it is blatantly offensive and you shouldn't go there

Member Definition

Make sure to have in black and white what exactly member privileges are. Each member should have a copy of this as should the team records contain a copy signed by each member stating they have read and understand the content. This could be considered a Member Contract.

As the team gets bigger and equipment is acquired and evidence collected and all kinds of stuff, this document might come in very handy should a member decide to leave the team or contest an action of another team member that they think is violating the member rules.

<u>This should be composed to not only protect the teams' rights but those of the member as well.</u>

Changes do happen. As revisions are made to this Member Contract, it doesn't hurt to have the members review and sign the revised contract. Think of it like a sports team and having a contract renewal and making sure everyone is on the same page.

RED FLAG

- One of the most common things heard out of a team member's mouth when confronted with a violation of the codes of conduct and/or member contract is the statement "I didn't know that". The gratification of having all your bases covered comes when you pull that copy out with their signature and show them they stated they read it and understood. Many times the next thing you hear is "I forgot." At least that lets the member know that the contract is for a purpose and not just to waste paper

Member Recruiting and Selection

Potential members can come from anywhere: work associate, family, online chat room, friend of a friend of a friend. No matter if they are a close friend or stranger, treat this situation as you would a job interview and hiring. There has to be an understanding that there will be no favoritism and that existing team members will have a say in whether they will be accepted as members or not.

Pairs vs. Singles?

We all have a relationship status: single, married, single with partner, parent, friend, and son or daughter. No different for potential team members. It is not unusual to get pairs interested in joining your team. The statement "we want to share this experience together" is often stated as the reason for pairs seeking membership in paranormal teams. However, you need to treat each individual as a recruit UNRELATED to the person they came with. Make this clear from the start.

If they aren't willing to go this route, then they probably aren't worth having on the team. If the person standing on their own will not fit within your team, how would being part of a duo make them fit?

Should each member pass team interviews and probation, there should be no problem having them as team members. However, if only one passes, the offer of team membership should be conveyed only to the individual passing. If they choose not to accept because the other person wasn't than that is their choice.

RED FLAGS

- Interview potential members away from other recruits. If a person came with others they may have practiced answers to questions. If you get them away from the influence of the other person, you might get some natural answers instead of practiced.

  Unfortunately some people will say things and act the way they think you want them to and not be their true selves. It's hard to filter these out. But, if you don't catch them early on you can find that later their real personalities and beliefs will only cause strife within the team

- When members of the team consist of couples in intimate relationships, make sure they understand that on team time they are to conduct themselves in a respectable manner. The last thing you need is video evidence showing team members making out on an investigation
- If you don't make member selection by discussion and vote of the existing team members, that immediately causes discord within the exiting team whether the candidate is made a member or not. Make sure existing members state all concerns up front and that they are addressed accordingly. These would be flagged as areas to watch during the probation

The team should have a brief bullet list of those traits the team is hunting for in a member. A set list of interview questions would also be a handy tool. As time goes one I'm sure that list will get longer and longer. However, the more you find out about a person up front the better decision the team can make as to either accepting or denying their membership.

RED FLAG

- Some questions might be viewed by the candidate as an invasion of privacy or too personal. The basic questions:
    - Do you take drugs (prescription and/or recreational)?
    - Do you drink alcohol?
    - Do you have a history of mental illness?
    - Have you ever been diagnosed with Bi-polar disorder?

    Can invoke anger from a candidate. Before asking such questions (which you really need to) explain to them the reason: On an investigation, other people's lives may depend upon yours. The team needs to know that you can be depended upon to be responsive and show up to client locations sober.

Also, although it is not hard facts, personal experiences and feelings at an investigation site are important tools. The team needs to know that a personal experience is real and not the results of hallucination.

If they do not want to answer such questions, this actions needs to be taken into consideration when the team makes their decision.

If they do answer the questions, but answers are negative, DO NOT PASS JUDGEMENT on them. It's not your place. Just make it clear again how what they are doing could impact the team negatively.

Unfortunately where prescription drugs are concerned we can't down a person for that as their health is of the utmost concern. However, knowing there is a medical condition is of benefit should the individual be accepted on the team and fall ill while on an investigation.

After interview(s) when the existing team votes, if it is in favor of the candidate, that should mean they are on the team but under probation.

If the candidate does NOT pass the team interview, the candidate deserves to know the reason(s). It is best for one of the existing team members to address the candidate and allow them to ask questions. You do not want them to feel ganged up on. Regardless of the candidate response, the decision cannot be revoked without the candidate going through the interview process with the entire team again.

Candidate Probation Period

Once the candidate has made it through the interview it's time to see how they are in action and how they interact and play with others. Being on probation means the individual is a team member and must follow all team rules and regulations.

Make sure your team by-laws state a set duration for probation (2-6 months, etc.). During this time any items that came up during the interview as possible concerns should be watched. Also make sure the probation portion of the by-laws covers non-compliance with team codes and rules. The common rule is that if a probationary member violates any of the rules or codes of conduct it is immediate cause for expulsion from the team.

During the probation period permanent members should keep notes on how they feel the probationary member's doing. They should also note any negative experiences. These might come into play should the individual be asked to leave at the end of the probation.

Probation should be done with one new member at a time. If they have to wait for another to go through their probation, that is an additional test of their will to be on the team and their patience. This type of limitation gives the existing team total control and full concentration in determining if that individual fits the team without having outside influences other than the norm.

The team needs to be firm and not afraid of hurting feelings when there is a candidate that doesn't fit the team. Be honest. If the team finds the candidate is not a fit for the team more than likely the candidates experience with the team would not be a pleasant one if allowed to become permanent.

RED FLAGS

- DO NOT cut the probation period short no matter how well the candidate fits in. If they fit in that well with the team and you're anxious to make them permanent, just be patient, the probation will not matter and it will be a real celebration when it is over and they are permanent
- On the other hand if they really aren't fitting in well, remember, you have accepted them enough to make them a probationary member. Unless they agree that they are not a fit with the team and sign a probation release you have to give them the entire time. Team them with a permanent member and make sure to document any violations of the rules or code of conduct
- Multiple individuals coming in together may show you only what they want you to see and there may be ulterior motives. Again, evaluate each individual and not the group
- Don't let the team make their decisions on here-say. Whatever happened with an individual on another team or outside of the team should not impact the teams' decision. Only what was witnessed during the interviews and the probation period should be used to make the decision whether the individual is invited as a permanent member

Member Probation

Sometimes things just happen that may make team members decide that one or more team members have fallen below team standards and/or are causing issues within the team infrastructure. Not to be used loosely or vindictively, probation is a means for team members to let their fellow members know that action needs to be taken to resolve either a performance or personality issue. Like new member probation, this should be documented in the by-laws and/or codes of conduct.

Have a form that members can use to submit their reasons for submitting another member for probation. If there is more than one being reported, each should be treated individually.

This may sound cruel but the accusing member should bring the form to the next business meeting of the team and bring it up as a new item. By having to announce this in front of the team it serves two-fold. 1.) The accuser will definitely make sure and feel strongly they have valid reasons. 2.) The accused will be able to state their case for the team to hear. There will be no "he said, she said" going on. The entire team will be aware of all that happens and is said.

Once the accuser brings this issue up, a mediator should be appointed by the team. The mediator should not be accused or accuser.

During the discussion the mediator should make sure tempers are kept down and emotions don't get the best of people. Basically they need to make sure the team sticks to the facts. The mediator should set a time of discussion (10-15 minutes) and take notes of the actions. At the end of the discussion time, the team, minus the accuser and accused, should vote on whether probation is necessary or not. Maybe the accusation was warning enough and no additional obedience is needed.

If the team members voting decide probation is valid, they must decide the duration and actions expected of the probie in order to successfully complete the probation without further disciplinary action. This should be documented by the mediator. The accused can either accept the decision of the team or additional action can be taken resulting in the accused being removed from investigations and/or the team entirely.

During the probation period, other members should keep notes on how they feel the probie's doing and if they are completing the actions required to conclude the probation period successfully.

RED FLAG

- Team Divas are no fun and not good for team stability. As the team develops and as the years go by, one or more members may shine above others. That is great but it doesn't give them rights to develop attitudes. It may take a member probation to bring them back to earth

Member Termination

If the Member probation doesn't work, the remaining team members have the authority to evict a member from the team for valid reasons. This would mean the conditions needing completed by the accused when put on probation were not met.

Violation of certain codes of conduct may be reasons for immediate expulsion from the team. These codes of conduct should specify this as a penalty for violation. An example of this would be deliberate destruction of a client location caught on video. That would be immediate eviction. In this instance there would be No vote, no discussion. If there was a witness and/or the action was caught on one of the video/DVR recorders, which is proof enough.

Unless it is immediate termination resulting from a violation of the codes of conduct, termination of a member should be done with a vote. The member being voted on does not have a vote. Document the reasons and notify the member of the results. Regardless if they are at the meeting or not, written notification is the best media so there is no doubt.

RED FLAGS

- Don't let one bad experience keep the team from being open to opportunities. Whether a candidate failed or an existing member turned sour, let it go and move on. Just because this happened once doesn't mean it will happen every time. Yes, it might happen again. But, between these failures you might find that diamond, a member that is hard working and brings several assets to the team
- Having a member kicked off (sorry no other way to put it nicely) may cause a disruption in the existing team

structure. It may even make other members choose to leave as well. Accept this as "Stuff Happens" and move on to strengthen the team

Personalities

RED FLAGS... RED FLAGS....RED FLAGS!!!!!!!

How can you fight human nature? Not everyone agrees with everyone else and just some people don't get along. This can be the biggest issue for any relationship whether it is a team, marriage, work or social relationship. The key thing to remember here is "DRAMA KILLS!!!!" Don't delay in handling a situation. The longer it goes on the more it festers and impacts the team. Use the member probation as a means of bringing the issue forward and coming to a successful solution.

Having various personalities on a team is why it is important to take time when adding a new member to make sure there is a fit. All it takes is one person to upset the entire team.

The Good and the Bad

There are as many personalities as there are people. Certain traits or beliefs of an individual can serve as a dual edge sword, good and bad. However, be open and not judge a person based on their religion, race, sexual orientation, occupation or another other criteria. Variety in member backgrounds adds knowledge and possible paranormal experiences.

The list is almost infinite but those listed here are common influences.

Skepticism

Regardless if it's spelled "skepticism" or "scepticism", there are so many definitions. However, in general it is defined as "any questioning attitude towards knowledge, facts, or opinions/beliefs stated as facts, or doubt regarding claims that are taken for granted elsewhere."[7]

Every team needs their skeptics. This provides a point of view for the team that others on the team may not realize. If there is not a skeptic on the team, believe me, there are plenty of skeptics outside the team that will be ready to rip evidence and anything brought to the table apart. Think of it as a goal. If a skeptic ever says either "I don't know" or "I believe", something is probably there.

RED FLAG

- On the other hand, having individuals that are so closed off or that will not open themselves up to new experiences can be a negative impact to the team

Criticism

The general public performs the art of criticism, "the practice of judging the merits and faults of something or someone in an intelligible way"[8].

The team and team members need to have thick skin. This is a field that feeds critics with all kinds of openings.

Positive and negative feedback should first come from within the team in preparation for what will be received from outside via web postings, reveals, conferences, etc. Take nothing

---

[7] As defined in Wikipedia, The Free Encyclopedia

[8] As defined in Wikipedia, The Free Encyclopedia

personal. Be honest and up front with your fellow team members. Especially during evidence analysis, be honest. If a presented EVP doesn't sound like anything, say so. If it doesn't sound like the statement another member hears, say so. If the quack in the audio sounds likes a squeaky shoe, say so. There will probably be others who feel this way or it will open the others minds to new possibilities. In fact your client may hear something totally different than anyone on the team did.

In other words, everyone will be scrutinizing the evidence and with that comes the criticism.

With some evidence it is so easy to be blinded by it. Meaning, to some there is no other explanation than paranormal where others look at it and start asking questions. Don't take it personal. Answer all the questions. If a legitimate explanation other than paranormal comes out of it, be grateful. Keep in mind that everyone has a right to their own opinion. Don't look at criticism as a negative thing regardless if it comes from inside or outside the team. It is only directed at the evidence and gives us cause to one day provide evidence that cannot be criticized.

RED FLAG

- Misdirected criticism is a negative impact on the team. Everyone has their own way of doing things. Who's to say which is right if the results are the same? If team and member policies are being adhered to, this is not a subject for criticism

Ethics

Just as the team should have a code of conduct, each person lives by their individual code of ethics, what they feel is right and what is wrong. However, not all meld well together or work in a team environment. There are so many traits under this umbrella; honesty, respect, dependability, and trust are just a few.

RED FLAG

- Individual and team ethics cannot conflict. WARNING... getting on a soap box now..... for example.... Using the "F" word. My personal feeling is this is unnecessary and VERY disrespectful to those around you under any circumstance or condition. However, there are those that use it every other word and see no issue with it. I don't want my clients seeing evidence with a team member doing EVPs who can't speak a sentence without saying this word 3 times. If the code of conduct covers cussing and a member lets it fly without consideration, this is an example of conflicting ethics. And yes, I'm a 52 year old fogie.

Popularity & Publicity

15 minutes of fame is always nice. If the team is popular because of quality work and customer service that is awesome. That should definitely be a goal of every team.

With the paranormal being a popular topic of TV shows, movies and publications there are always opportunities for respected teams to get in the spotlight. This is when the team needs to examine carefully what their purpose is and what the future of the team is.

More and more teams are going to radio shows and pod casts. This is definitely the natural progression in the name of growth. However, with this also comes more dedication required from team members.

In open forum broadcasts or any time you are in front of the microphone and/or bright lights there is a lot of opportunity to share information with the public and work with those interested in the paranormal.

Blush.... It seems like just about every team has one or more members that want to write books. Sharing information is the best thing a person can do. Most of us love to learn new things and if we can read something that will keep us from making a mistake, we're happy to hear about it.

Just because you, your team and/or a team member has been in the paper, a magazine or book, on the radio or TV isn't justification to act "better than thou".

RED FLAG

- Be careful in broadcasts what investigation information is being disclosed. It is easy to get excited about those great investigations but sometimes those clients did not agree to go public. Just a slip of client name or location might cause serious confidentiality issues for the team

- Restraint needs to be practiced so that the wish for popularity doesn't impact the investigation and customer trust

Responsibilities and Roles within the Team

Just like in any business, roles (jobs) within the team need to be defined. This does not mean there is a one for one ratio here; or one person for each role.

Along with a title for each role, there also needs to be a "job description". This will define what the responsibilities are for a person in that role. A single team member can perform several roles. As the team gets bigger and expands services and/or territory more responsibilities may be involved.

Here are just a few examples of roles within a paranormal team:

- **Investigator** – All members of a team perform this role. Within this role, there could be different levels based on experience: Investigator I (rookie), Investigator II (1-5 years experience), Senior Investigator (6+ years experience)
- **Case Manager** – This can be a big job and time consuming. The individual(s) in this role is the first contact in most cases with the customer. They are responsible for booking cases and follow-up with potential clients. In many teams all members take on this role at one time or another
- **Technical Manager** – all team members should know the equipment and be able to perform in this aspect. However, having 1 person as a primary to track and maintain the equipment is smart
- **Historian** - Research is a key tool in investigating. All team members should assist in this area but having a primary is smart

- **Team Webmaster**– this person maintains the team website and keeps it up to date with events, investigations and other information the team chooses to post on the site
- **Team Secretary** – this person should take notes; maintain membership records and all forms and contracts. There needs to be one location for team records
- **Investigation Roles** – these roles pertain strictly to investigations. These should vary with each investigation so that all members become experienced in the positions and no one person becomes burned out having to fill that job EVERY time:
  - **Lead** – Primary customer contact and person who is responsible for all decisions in respect to this specific investigation
  - **Investigators** – Investigators assigned to this client
  - **Technical Setup** – There should be one person responsible for the site setup and tracking all equipment for an investigation. Everyone on the investigation should help set up and break down but decisions regarding equipment should be deferred to this individual. This is important so that all equipment is accounted for at the end of an investigation and when it is a factor in evidence there are a minimum number of influences

RED FLAGS

- Regardless of the job/role a team member takes, all members of the team are equal. Only the Founder or elected team leader has the right to rule the roost…. Within team guidelines and codes of course!

- If a team member has no time for investigations, they definitely wouldn't have time for other positions within the team

- Team is a part of teamwork. Some of the roles within the team are a lot of work. All members should be willing to help when asked. If they don't know how to do something they should be willing to learn

Chapter 3. Establishment

As stated under "Conception", there are resolutions that need to be made either at the beginning or after you have a core team. The following are just a few key decisions:

Democratic Infrastructure vs. Dictatorship

Who's in charge?   Will one individual, the founder or appointed individual, act as a president and be responsible for making decisions for the team or will it be a democratic system where you might have one individual leading the meetings but all decisions are made as a team, with majority rules?

If being totally democratic or totally dictatorial does not fit your teams' ideal leadership structure, there is a meet halfway, or compromise management arrangement. You can maintain your leadership and control of the team by stating clearly that as founder you hold the controls of organizational decisions and standards.   However, the Team can be democratic in investigation and membership decisions.

RED FLAG

- How your team will be managed is a serious issue that cannot be easily changed later if at all. As founder this could also be a judgment of your integrity. If you choose to maintain some control of all actions don't doubt you will be called up regarding some issue or another and maybe even challenged as to what decisions you've made.

Dues vs. No Dues

This is a touchy subject. Some teams use this as a means to filter those really serious vs. individuals just out for the fun of it. It is also a way to finance investigations and equipment.

Whether your team does or doesn't charge dues, make sure it is documented clearly. If it does, specify amount and frequency. Make sure there is no doubt.

If your team requires dues:

- It is advised a checking account under the team name be opened and 2-3 member signatures required for check endorsement or any type of transaction
- A team ledger showing dues paid and when member's dues are due should be maintained so that there is financial accountability.

RED FLAGS

- In your team By-Laws there should be a separate section relating to dues and if a member falls in arrears
- A very picky subject is "Are dues refundable?" Make sure this is covered in your by-laws. Members choosing to leave the team might ask for refund for unexpired dues

Team Assets and Equipment

Once your team is established and acquires equipment and items under the team name, you should have a ledger of all equipment and assets owned by the team. I advise documenting serial numbers where applicable and purchase values.

You may never need this information but as we all know, some of the equipment is expensive. Should the location where it is being stored by damaged or broken into, this information will be valuable to have for insurance purposes.

Also, it doesn't hurt to have a fiscal accounting for the team and its assets and expenses in general. Keep in mind this doesn't just mean equipment used for investigations. It could mean office supplies and anything used in the operation of the team.

Any utility expenses such as phones should also be noted. Many teams just use personal phones under individual team members. It might not be a bad idea to get a prepaid phone like Tracfone, Net 10 or any non-contract phone. This will keep the monthly expense down. By having a dedicated line for client calls you can have an idea of what activity the team has every month.

An additional expenditure may be web hosting fees. If you pay anything for your web site, that should be a team expense.

You'd be amazed at the number of expenses a team can accrue. By documenting and logging the team will be more aware of team assets.

RED FLAG

- Any assets of the team need to be accounted for and figures readily available to all team members. If any expenditure under the team name is made, there should be corresponding documentation. You never know when you will be questioned regarding it by internal and/or external parties. It's nice to be able to pull out a record and state, "that DVR was purchased on such and such date at this store..... No it wasn't out of the back of a truck."

Equipment in General

Equipment used in paranormal research and investigation is a subject that could be the bases for a class and/or book of its own. It will be discussed here at a high level In relation to the team and its function.

A primary resource for any paranormal team is the equipment used for investigations. This can be vast and expensive.

When a team first starts out, equipment used during investigations may be only that which is personally owned by the individual members. After the team has stabilized, there may come a time when each member pitches in or membership dues are used for purchasing team equipment.

All members should be familiar with each piece of equipment used. That's not saying they have to be experts. However, knowledge of how to properly use each piece is necessary for consistent results in evidence capture.

RED FLAG

- Many times, members will gift the team with equipment and/or money to purchase equipment for the team. Regardless of which, a receipt from the team secretary/administrator needs to be given to the member doing the gifting. That receipt should also be initialed by the gift giver. A duplicate/copy of that receipt should be filed in the team records. Should questions arise regarding equipment ownership, this will provide validation

Team Documentation and Forms

There is no one perfect set of these for all teams. Each team needs a set based on the founders' dreams and expectations and those expectations and ideas of the chartered team.

Instead of giving an example here that may or may not fit your needs, I advise going online, search and review several examples to find what fits your team. It may be a combination of many.

If you use the following search criteria you will see a lot out there. Using an internet browser such as Google here are some suggested queries:

- For a Mission Statement search for "Paranormal Mission Statement"
- For a Code of Conduct search for "Paranormal code of conduct"
- For By-Laws search for "Paranormal By-Laws"
- For a Member Contract search for "Paranormal Member Contract"
- For a Client Application search for "Paranormal Client Application"
- For Liability forms search for "Paranormal Liability"

Don't stop at these. There are other documents that can be used also. It is all a matter of how thorough you want to document your team. Just keep in mind that form, rule, restriction, code, by-law, etc..... Is a means of protecting the team and/or each member from themselves and external strife.

Here are brief descriptions of common documents and forms:

Mission Statement

A brief statement of what the team does, for who and how it is done. This statement should be supported by all members of the team.

Code of Conduct

A set of conventional principles and expectations that are considered binding on any person who is a member of the team. Penalties for violations of these should also be stated.

By-Laws

The rules and regulations enacted by team to provide a framework for its management and operation. In other words, it is the rules governing the internal affairs of the team.

Legal Forms

In this day and age, unfortunately one of the important things is CYT, Cover Your Team. You need to protect your team members from one another, your clients from team members, your team members from clients and just in general have it all wrapped in a nice documented bundle…. With signatures.

Member Contract

All members of the team should have a signed contract on file with the team secretary. The Member Contract should outline what being a member involves. A copy of the teams Code of Conduct and By-Laws should also be included and initialed by the member signifying they have read them and agree with them. Validation that they have read these and understand them is important.

Client Liability

Prior to investigating a location, the client responsible for that location must complete and sign a liability release. This protects the team from any accidents happening on site. This should be included with the completed client interview form.

Team Liability

Prior to investigating a location, all members of the team that will step on the premises being investigated will be required to sign a liability release. This protects the client from any accidents happening on site.

RED FLAG

- Without appropriate forms completed, the team could be held liable for damage and injuries during an investigation. No matter how well intended the team is to help a client, they also need to protect the team from any legal repercussions. Unfortunately there are those people out there that take glory in pulling a scam over teams such as paranormal teams

Team Publicity

How will the team be advertised? If it will be with a web site, a web master will have to be found or members volunteer to fill that role. The team should agree on the functionality of the site and appearance.

Meetings

Communication is important to any relationship, especially one where multiple members are involved. Phone calls, texts and emails are great ways of keeping abreast of things as they happen, but meeting in person and having an interactive conversation is the best to get business taken care of.

How often will the team meet and duration of meetings?

These factors may vary as evidence review meetings are called which can take time. But a standing team meeting to discuss team business should be decided on.

RED FLAG

- This is a main place where the team will interfere with each member's personal life. A majority of your members will probably hold full time jobs or manage households. This in itself leaves little time for other stuff. Dedicating at least an hour on a regular basis just for a meeting might be difficult to schedule. Be understanding when meetings fall on dates when family functions are happening or work calls

Meetings can also easily stray to non-team related subjects. Make sure to have the team administrator/secretary make an agenda of business needing covered. Follow this agenda. For those wishing to socialize about other things, they can do so after the business meeting has concluded. It's best to keep the business aspect of the meeting to around an hour.

Where do we meet?

Not many teams are lucky enough to have a facility entirely dedicated to the team operation. That leaves public places or members residences. If all of your members live in the same area it works well to take turns hosting. Otherwise a centralized location might be favorable. Of course there are always other factors that might come into play such as technical needs (i.e. does the location have internet), privacy and weather.

RED FLAG

- CELL PHONES... sigh! During the meeting it is best to have a rule regarding cell phones and texting. Distractions like this can prevent participation in the meeting. Unless a member is on call with work and must have their phone on it is best all members silence their phones and no texting allowed

Evidence Ownership

All audio, video, photography, etc. should be turned over immediately after an investigation to the team secretary. This ensures no evidence is lost and that all can be reviewed for client reveal. Things happen and team members drop or have things come up and can't review the evidence they captured. It is still the teams' responsibility to review this for the client.

The following guidelines are followed by some teams:
- The Team will always be an owner of the evidence
- Based on client liability contract

- o If client allows evidence and their identity to be used publicly than client has limited say so in use. However, as a business courtesy keep client informed of use
- o If client does not allow evidence and identity disclosed, they become co-owners with the team
- As a member of the team and acting under the team name during the capture of the evidence, this forfeits the individual members claim as owner. However, credit can be given to the individual on behalf of the team as "photo captured by John Doe" ... etc. The individual will be trusted to treat the evidence with confidentiality if they still maintain a personal copy

RED FLAG

- If a member leaves the team (for whatever reason) and confidential evidence is disclosed, this could make for some unhappy clients and controversy over the team ethics. This is why a team member contract would be important that states basically – upon separation from team the individual will not disclose confidential information such as client list and evidence under penalties of legal action

Chapter 4. Operation

Once the team is defined, staffed and rules (so to say) are established it is time for the functionality or operation of the team. This is another area that can be a document all its own[9] and for each team this will vary. The operation of the team is based on all decisions made during conception and establishment. With the documentation maintained in these steps, it will be easy to establish rules of operation:

- Definition of Services Offered
- Rules of Investigation
- Client Evaluation Procedure
- Evidence Review Procedure
- Client Reveal Procedure
- Operational Procedures (i.e. maintaining case histories, equipment maintenance, etc.)

All members must know and understand these.

Parting Words

In conclusion, here are just a few recommendations to each member. These will aid in maintaining a successful team:

- Be organized in the team operation and for investigations. Organization makes for smooth setup and breakdown
- Be professional
- Respect your fellow team members, the client and the location – remember that what you say and do during an investigation will show up on audio and video
- Practice control - Keep cool, watch your language and convey confidence to the client

---

[9] hmmm.. perhaps next in the Red Flag Series

- Don't take it personal. Evidence you have captured will be criticized and torn apart. Be open to others opinions
- Be honest, dependable and flexible
- Don't hold grudges. If you have an issue with the team or a team member, bring it out in the open and get it resolved. All members must get along

GOOD LUCK!

www.ingramcontent.com/pod-product-compliance
Lightning Source LLC
Chambersburg PA
CBHW060007300526
45794CB00003B/1131